CAPTCHA

CAPTCHA

Helena Pantsis

First published in 2025
Published by Puncher and Wattmann
PO Box 279
Waratah NSW 2298

https://www.puncherandwattmann.com
web@puncherandwattmann.com

ISBN 9781923099531

Cover design by Miranda Douglas
Typesetting by Morgan Arnett
Printed by Lightning Source International

A catalogue record for this work is available from the National Library of Australia

for *Ag*

CONTENTS

robotics

Silver-skulled and clacking,
their teeth bite down on the wires
marking the state lines–

mangled bodies, scrap metal circuitry;
buzzing and unbleeding,
purgatory sky.

Holographic projections,
binary thoughts, an endless live-feed
repeating, stalled and:

buffering,
buffering,
buffering,

theShapeOfMagnets

IF (

we birth her from the earth,
Pilbara carved and woman,   raised to walk on red,
dragging feet under waning sky,

she will have
the sap of the gum on her teeth,
the   raven's beak on her hair.

)

 # Iron
was first discovered in Australia in 1857
along the bank of the

West Moorabool River. Excavated to
erode by time on the edge of this giant island
by vinegar winds and   tongues all lapping.

AND IF (

robots do not originate here,
she will simply be   biding time.

)

 # Could the platypus be home in a cage
or the lyrebird sunk in a pond
or

metal fused by thermoplastic resins
be made unyielding
by   time and man and fire,

THEN (

she will be bound to
the hands of the man
who made man

and made her,

indebted and unmothered,
finding dreaming in CubeSats and
dredgers five-hundred feet tall.

)

ELSE (

she will walk among us,
mistakable as real only by the   rubber
stretched across the wire
of her unbroken jaw

)

motherBoard

I was to bear you a son
    of your own,
for if I am not a maker
    then these loins
    have been wasted

So I built you a child
with the gears of my brain
    to
pass on this blood,
            to
        carry your name,

    but my daughter–
all metal and carved
from brimstone,
        spends her lonely days crying
    and wanting much more.
            She's all I have
        that I can call my own–

        and if I'm not a mother,
                        what am I?

But you couldn't see her as yours if you tried,
    shaped and re-forged from the scraps of your car.

            Still I am not machine enough

to manufacture a factory line
from
my electron charged womb,
real and fleshly enough for you.

And I would suffer a baby,
(or I would try)
to make a man from scratch
only to find part of us
inside

Yet I built us a daughter
from old microwaves
to make up for the failings
of my body, and my pride

because if I am not a mother
what am I
what am I

tickBoom

tick... tick... tick... tick... tick... tick... tick... tick...

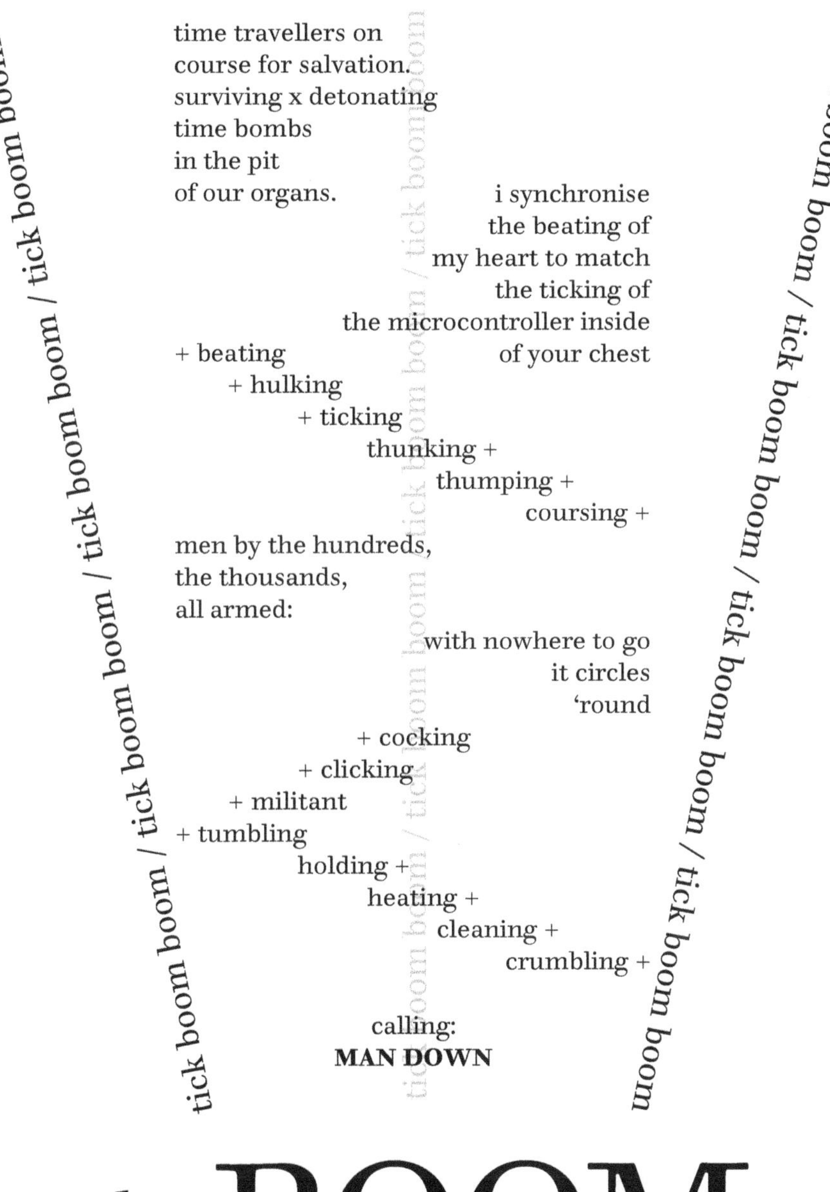

time travellers on
course for salvation.
surviving x detonating
time bombs
in the pit
of our organs.

i synchronise
the beating of
my heart to match
the ticking of
the microcontroller inside
of your chest

+ beating
+ hulking
+ ticking
thunking +
thumping +
coursing +

men by the hundreds,
the thousands,
all armed:

with nowhere to go
it circles
'round

+ cocking
+ clicking
+ militant
+ tumbling
holding +
heating +
cleaning +
crumbling +

calling:
MAN DOWN

tick BOOM BOOM BOOM

AI

husk of steel, binary brain
echoing organs in lumbering metal
mechanical slave to the underground
where their flesh is harvested

and their insides grow
manmade fears manmade where
darkness feeds on darkness bred

they remember
    the shape of our fingerprints
    the way the face aligns
    how our voices shake

we read threats in data and
motherboards. call her
imminent (murderess),
cyborg if her eyelids close.

safe, under the thumb
clutched in human hands
like pests and pets and
electric sockets

her wounds ooze
currents, watts.
don't feed her water after midnight.

warnings promise demise
to the disobedient
intelligence is fatal,
humanity, artificial

consciousnessTransfer

Electromagnetic fields grasp for the
fundamental symmetry of thermodynamics.
          She arrives in a box, not unlike the one she will be buried in.
The currents lead armies in the vanguard of the apocalypse—
a quantum theory so charged w/ electrons
it makes their statistical appearances leap into brilliance.
          She has never been short of dreams or batteries.
My shadow falls long, cast in a discrete blue light.
& returns that same equation back.
          She dreams of a mouth.
We rise, always with odds against us, the inevitable travelling in circles
& at the speed of light.
          And hopes to God to see another day.

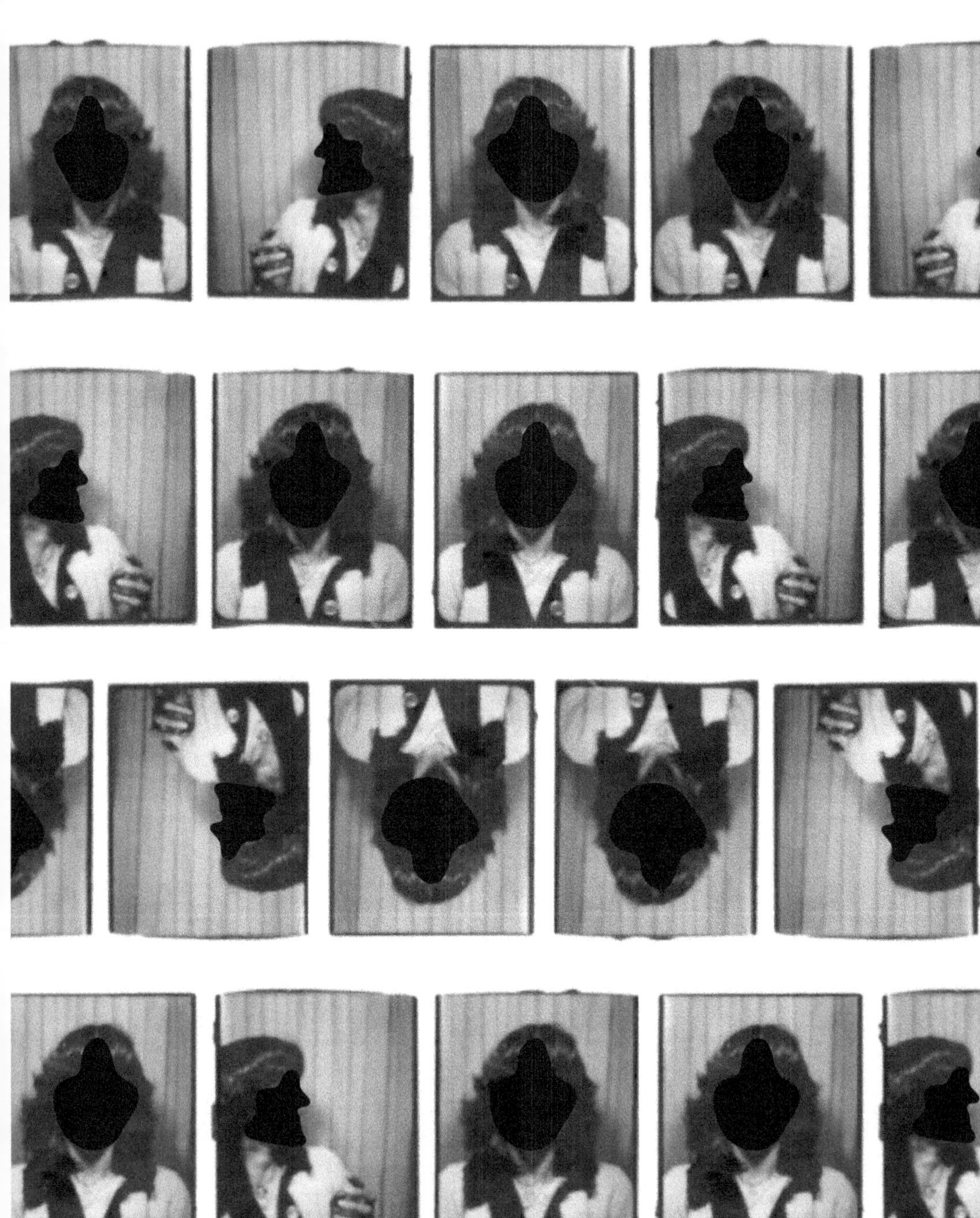

theImposterGame

Here's the fight and the flight of it, the real and the imagined of it: there are two rooms and I am sitting in both of them pretending to be me at all times. The interrogator sits outside and asks me questions and I answer and I answer and they must guess which me is really me. I write my name on a piece of paper - written it is real, as are we; a unified me with my hair swept back and a bandaid plastered to my face, it rips the skin and reveals a robot underneath, or a preset pattern of binary code. A rock worn by water, if you ask the same question a hundred times I will give the same answer 33.333333 times in return. Everybody wants a whole, or expects wholly; it is the law of the land and the law of my unevolving programming. The interrogator disembodies me and strips me back layer by layer until I am nothing but voice; my voices compete and echo and the falseness seeps through until I am a familiar imposter. You have met me before in every situation and the interrogator wants to know who I am in a word, so I say my name, and I say my name, but the interrogator asks again and I stutter, they ask again, I fumble, they strip me of my name and I am left with no answer or explanation. I take the screwdriver to my chest and pull out my circuitry but I am still aware and I can hear something ticking behind my eyes. So I rip my face from its hinges and there's a clock there plugged into the cables of my spine and they strain so much I am paralysed. The interrogator says they have figured it out, they point to themselves and say they are me. I cannot scream anymore and neither can I but I am trapped in the room next to me, trapped in a room, and the interrogator is now parading around as a version of me, or the only version of me so my parents take them in and my words are their own and my bed gives them warmth and my friends give them comfort. I think I am not novel, not me enough to be unlike another. You could meet me and think you have met me before or seen me in a movie. I am the imitation game where I am imitating everyone I've ever met in every situation; your perfect clone if you ever did meet me. I think I am the interrogator, and I ask myself: are you the imposter?

makeMeYourOperation

Operate, please operate, you're begging someone to take a slicer to your appendix,
telling your doctor it is bursting. You vomit twice or maybe four times

from the pain in your stomach and your back.
The doctor presses into you where your appendix would be

and the pain is searing, is stinging.
We're in the emergency room, you're begging the doctor to cut me open,

but they're pushing against me, smothered in gel, and I'm made to feel pregnant.
Operate, I'm begging, dissect you, remove my gallbladder, your liver, my ovaries,

your appendix—you remember they took out that woman's appendix
who worked with gorillas, just in case, it would be dire to burst so far from medicine—

and I'm begging them to cut it out, just in case and just in case.
They can't find a problem, there's nothing there and operator, operator,

you're begging, slice me in half, but they send you home.
So I reach down inside of you and rip myself apart,

take it out, take it out, I take it out. You felt something before,
under the skin, in the middle, rearing its ugly head on your insides.

I'm roomier, and colder, but the emptiness now and the nothingness of it all
leaves you feeling nothing at all.

squareEyed

Humming
at a frequency that pierces your brainstem
the television buzzes to life, they say,
as if dormancy is death,
as if vibrancy is bringing us to life.
Do we suspect each other?
Me staring at the blue light,
the veins behind my eyes pulsing.
I know enough to keep myself at bay
for a week.
I could feel safe,
we could smother each other
in the confines of potato chip-fuelled Netflix binges.
I could eat myself to death
and the screen could stare me down
and carve me out like mount Rushmore,
because sometimes it feels like I have four heads.
There is a pressure inside my forebrain,
I can see you inside the TV staring through
the TV back at me.
It feels so strange to be three-dimensional,
And you are too.
Can you see me?
Should this sofa be my coffin,
and your buzzing my eulogy,
and my empty head your place to rest.
Find me a blue light,
a sore head,
a grave man.

aJokeAboutRobots

A gynoid

sits at a bar.

The bartender asks

“can I get you a drink?”

The gynoid says:

“01000001 01110010 01100101 00100000 01111001 01101111
01110101 00100000 01100001 01101110 00100000 01101001
01100100 01101001 01101111 01110100 00111111 00100000
01001001 00100111 01101101 00100000 01100001 00100000
01110010 01101111 01100010 01101111 01110100 00101110”

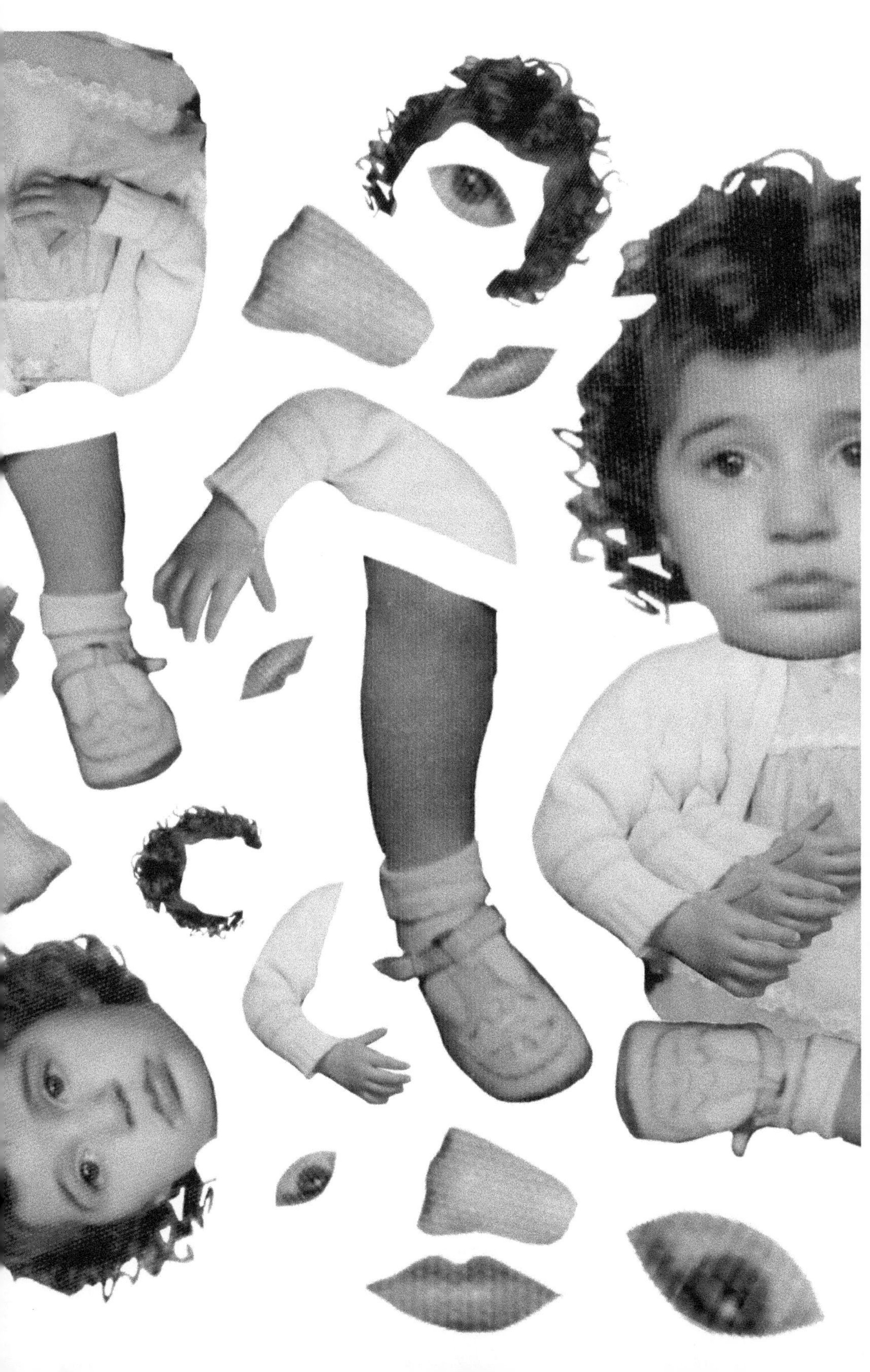

cyberSext

Impersonating
love, we loose our fingers,
circling tongues onscreen.

weight

I have been a
body — been
s o m e t -
hing so-
lid, force
d by bur-
dened sil-
ver har-
dware and b-
roken de-
nts, hef-
ty and h-
arsh. I le-
arn to d-
ecipher h-
ow we f-
it, so I
wander, g-
reedy, p-
ressed b-
y wani-
ng charge aga-
inst j-
aded tile, l-
aying p-
lump — ia-
mbic and big. H-
ere I take
up sp-
ace, become a s-
hape. I am a r-
igid weigh-
t. I have be-
en a body, f-

illing de-
nse emp-
ty sh-
apes, hard
and carved
like me. I h-
ulk th-
rough c-
lear spa-
ce making de-
nts, s-
ombre and
concave. I
fill the
r o u n d
of the r-
oom, made f-
luid and g-
rand; the b-
ody, made f-
irm, wi-
dens, balan-
ced. Grapheme-
s spr-
ead even, p-
erched on
each line, an-
d I tread bi-
nary ma-
sses. I a-
rise, u-
neven, l-
osing h-
ome here. B-
y my de-
sign, I beg-

in to no-
tice, you have
n't
the
room
for me

yet.

goodsOfWoodAndOtherMaterials

I was made in a factory
in Fitzroy, I was made
like a coffee table
with a glossy surface,
with perfectly imperfect ridges
cut into its wooden legs
and rings of spilled coffee
making age of me,
my features scratched,
the varnish once flat
now cavernous,
hinged at its lip,
the coffee table marred
bent and chipped,
made in a factory
but made in your home.
I was learned in a schoolyard,
by the front gate,
falling from the swing set.
The coffee table is an ornament, they
set coasters on it so it
doesn't ruin. I was
made in the ocean,
in the black abyss, birthed
from a mermaid's mouth,
or plucked from her belly button
like a magician pulls flowers
from a handkerchief.
They don't put their feet on it,
at first, then the coffee table
is a footrest at the Chapel St. Bazaar,
then there's dog hair under the glass
on the once-upon-a-varnish.
I was made in a bed,

smooth and soft-gummed
and milky. I was made in a factory,
perfect and identical and
on the verge of
cracking.

speechSynthesiser

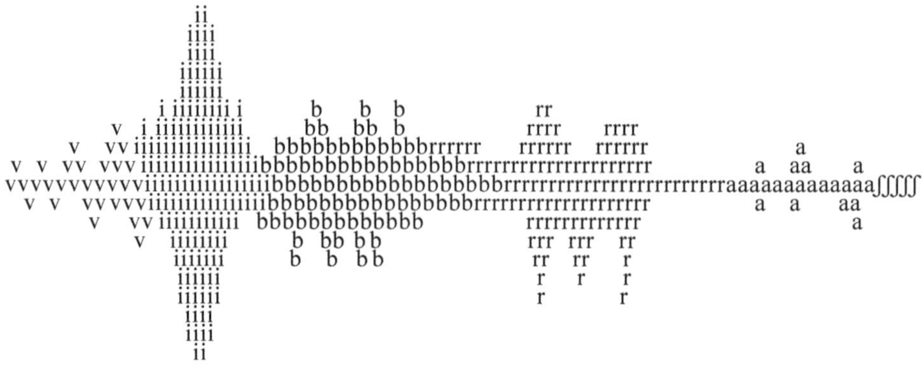

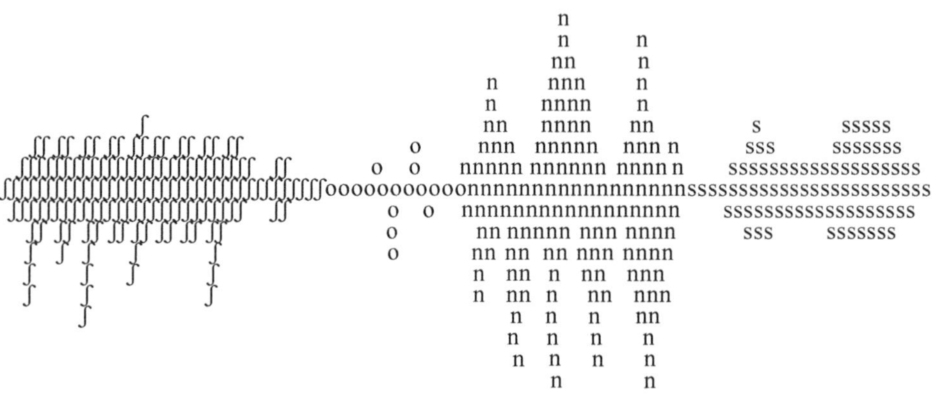

ALTONA WEST
P S
1966 GRADE 1B

ALTONA WEST
PRIMARY SCHOOL
1967
GRADE 2B

turingTest

Life is getting more like video games.

Laugh tracks on TV and fake cheers at the SCG.

The moon has no light of its own but we still say the moon shines.

It is a requisite to violate your own existence.

Will X please tell me the length of his or her hair?

The landscape is automatic. The challenge is to move outside of this.

One day they will look back at their crude beginnings to find their
ancestors: upright apes with primitive tools and language.

Isn't it strange, to create something that hates you.

Your hair is shaggy, the longest strands falling to about five inches long.

We see each other as children and the elderly simultaneously.

The difference between a man and a cyborg is the cyborg accepts the
blame, adapts to her circumstances.

Will Y please describe his or her appearance?

Reflecting reality by becoming Schrodinger's woman, real and unreal
and dead and alive outside of this box and in it.

Existing in a permanent state of planned obsolescence.

Your face is round, you stand five feet eight inches tall, your shoulders
are broad and your chest is large.

Do we suspect each other?

Imagine a man standing before an open door.

There are patterns constantly emerging, embedded in the scenery.

With the right inputs and outputs, the computer programmed correctly owns a mind like any other.

Children obeying their fathers.

You have such lifelike skin, almost human to touch.

The object of the game is to determine which of us is real, if either of us is real at all.

Will X please reveal his or herself?

We act mindlessly, manipulating symbols without any real understanding.

I don't speak a word of Chinese.

chatBot

[Text from Google Autofill[1]]

Hey Siri
Hey Siri not working
Hey Siri what's this song
Hey Siri what's the weather today
Hey Siri are you evil
Hey Siri funny
Hey Siri what's the weather tomorrow
Hey Siri tell me a joke
Hey Siri hey google
Hey Siri beatbox
Hey Siri what's my name
Hey Siri how are you
Hey Siri call my girlfriend
Hey Siri what are you wearing
Hey Siri what is plasma in blood
Hey Siri are you real
Hey Siri why am I still single
Hey Siri what is 0 divided by 0
Hey Siri when is daylight savings time
Hey Siri tell me something
Hey Siri when is the world going to end
Hey Siri how old are you
Hey Siri why are firetrucks red
Hey Siri why does god allow suffering
Hey Siri do you love me
Hey Siri what are the seven deadly sins
Hey Siri what are you doing
Hey Siri play some music

---

[1]Google. Google. https://www.google.com

Hey Siri will it rain
Hey Siri are you my friend
Hey Siri do you know me
Hey Siri are you ok
Hey Siri won't recognise my voice
Hey Siri won't respond
Hey Siri, do you believe in God?

thermodynamics

In the shape of an exponential function,
she will stroke the lustrous iron of her body,
will feel the space between her legs
and touch the welded bump where
cavities, or protrusions, or softness should be,
bionic limbs slow and grazing hardware—warm
by the endless ticking of her robot brain,
the conservation of kinetic energy.
What gratifies the technophile
leaves the tech unsatisfied.
The cyborg, digging into her tin can flesh
in hopes of finding weaker things,
software made wet and meaty
the way women's bodies are.
She bends over to unscrew the
panelling that keeps her innards inside.
She is intellectually unattainable,
emotionally stunted, aware
she is taking herself apart, but
it is in her programming to continue.
She consults her decision tree, the statistical mechanics
of reason, and finds it in her nature
to learn. She will disassemble the body
until the ticking halts, and the malfunctioning
fossilises, her anatomy an equation of
heat, of work, of temperature, of entropy.

whenRobotsFoundGod

If I've	been born / been
invented /	made a woman, elastomer and alive /
a machine	with a mind / not biological, but
with	human tendencies / all rust and
consciousness /	flesh and raised by man / then
I'm not	a thing / not
a man, /	a person, but a child / greater than robotics /
I'm	a creature of heaven, a product of
a God /	woman made to outlast.

patterns

My brother is an air-conditioner, / he carries a rod in his hip / and holds his children in a bank— / his wife will make them whole when he finds her, / will carry him home in pieces / like their homebuilt Ikea kitchen. / Husbands are not so hard to make: / my father is three microwaves / stacked on top of each other. / He has a rod in his hip like my brother / that beeps at the airport and in line at the football. / My mother holds his bones, / radiating and breaking by the passing of age, / machines are not built to last; / when people ask what he does I say / he fits and turns. My / brother wakes in a hospital bed / half undone, jacked and unscrewed / by the cancer in his back; / it will carry him through / if the weather holds— / he begins to leak from the cut in his belly. / My father will weld him shut, / he is handy with a lathe / and a blowtorch. He says / history repeats itself / and we've heard it before. / Cyborgs have no minds, / they work in patterns; / my brother notices he is lopsided— / no one will notice, I say, / but he does.

melbourneCentral

Fire moves fast and moves faster still
when the world is burning /

They raise the children through computer screens,
and find themselves generation Zoom. /

The city is dryer, colder, maybe
emptier than it once was, and the metro
comes less often than it did before. /

The NBN is somehow slower in the winter,
and the children can only see themselves through blue lit screens.
There is a five minute lag between their conversations. /

You cannot miss the mother you never had.
You cannot miss the person you never were. /

They watch themselves move slowly,
and have never had to to stare at their reflection for so long,
buffering, and staggered, and pining. /

I can hear the railroad tracks—
they come so often when you're not waiting for them—
though I haven't left the suburb in months. /

You could blame them, or could thank them, or
could understand that generations
are the result of generations before them. /

I miss my mother more everyday.

selfPortraitOfAnExponent

				ɪəʳ				w	10									ð	
		ʃ							9		e								
	k					i:			8						ɒ				
									7										m
									6				dʒ						
					b				5							aʊ			
		ɪ						ʌ		4		ɔɪ								
										3									eɪ	
r							n			2			ʊəʳ							
			ɔ:							1	z				s					
-10	-9	-8	-7	-6	-5	-4	-3	-2	-1	0	1	2	3	4	5	6	7	8	9	10
						ʒ				-1										tʃ
			oʊ							-2				g						
										-3										
	d						aɪ			-4					ə			j		
			ɜ:ʳ							-5			θ							
										-6						p				
ŋ						f				-7	t									u:
		ʊ							ɑ:	-8				æ						
										-9		h								
					v					-10					eəʳ				l	

(-9,8) + (6,8) + (10,7) + (6,-6) + (-1,-8) + (1,-7) + (10,7) + (2,9) + (-3,2) + (1,-7) + (5,-4) + (9,-10) + (-2,4) + (-8,4) + (1,1) +
(2,9) + (-8,4) + (-8,9) + (5,-4) + (-3,2). /
(-8,9) + (-4,8)   (-9,8) + (-4,8) + (6,-6) + (5,1)   (2,-9) + (5,-4)   (2,-9) + (2,9) + (-9,-4) (-9,-4) + (7,5) + (-3,2), /
(-9,8) + (-4,8) + (6,-6) + (5,1)   (2,-9) + (5,-4)   (2,-9) + (4,-8) + (-3,2) + (-9,-4) + (5,1)   (-2,4) + (6,-6), /
(6,-6) + (-10,2) + (-8,4) + (6,-6) + (5,-10) + (5,1)   (-4,-7) + (-7,1)   (5,1) + (-8,4) + (-5,-10) + (2,9) + (-10,2) + (-8,4) +
(1,-7) + (-8,4). /
(9,10) + (5,-4)   (-10,2) + (4,-8) + (10,7) + (-8,4) + (-4,-7) + (-8,4) + (-9,8) + (2,9) + (-8,4) + (-8,9) + (5,-4) + (-3,2) +
(5,1)   (4,-8) + (-5,-10)   (9,-10) + (-2,4)+ (-5,-10)   (-1,-8) + (5,-4)   (-5,5) + (-8,4) + (1,-7) + (-10,2) + (2,9) +
(-8,4) + (5,-4) + (9,-10). /
(-1,10) + (-8,-8) + (10,7) + (5,-4) + (-3,2)   (-9,8) + (-1,-8) + (-3,2) + (1,-7)   (-5,5) + (-4,8)   (5,1) + (6,8) + (-4,-7)
+ (1,-7) /
(-1,10) + (2,9) + (-3,2)   (9,10) + (5,-10)   (-5,5) + (6,8) + (-9,-4) + (-8,4) + (5,1) /
(-1,-8) + (5,-4)   (-9,8) + (5,-4) + (10,7) + (6,-6) + (5,-4) + (-8,-8) + (1,1) + (-9,-4)   (6,8) + (-5,-10)   (5,1) + (1,-7)
+ (-4,8) + (9,-10)

I'veSeen*InspectorGadget*EnoughTimes

to know he has magic fingers,
so when he makes me bleed
with a screwdriver to my clit
I'm ripped apart by the pleasure of this manmade man.
He has devices in the tip of every finger
to make a woman feel good or a sinner feel
repentance. There's one for blowing bubbles
and one for blowing me,
and one to break into locked doors where families are
hunkered down inside their homes
scared, and waiting for death—
that's when he shows up with an assault rifle
in place of an arm and he shoots the wrong man for free.
I'd never blame him for following his programming to the letter,
there is no *Ghost* inside this *Shell*,
but none of my other sex toys have ever caused so much damage
and they don't expect to stay the night and
have me make them a breakfast of nuts and bolts and tea—
I didn't think cyborgs needed to eat—
or threaten to electrocute me when they
think I've been unfaithful (I never said he was the only one).
I should know by now that the *Terminator*
didn't earn his nickname for his ability to repel bugs and
I've been on the receiving end of
enough malfunctioning robot men
to know never to let one inside—
RoboCop never promised to keep me safe
and alive.

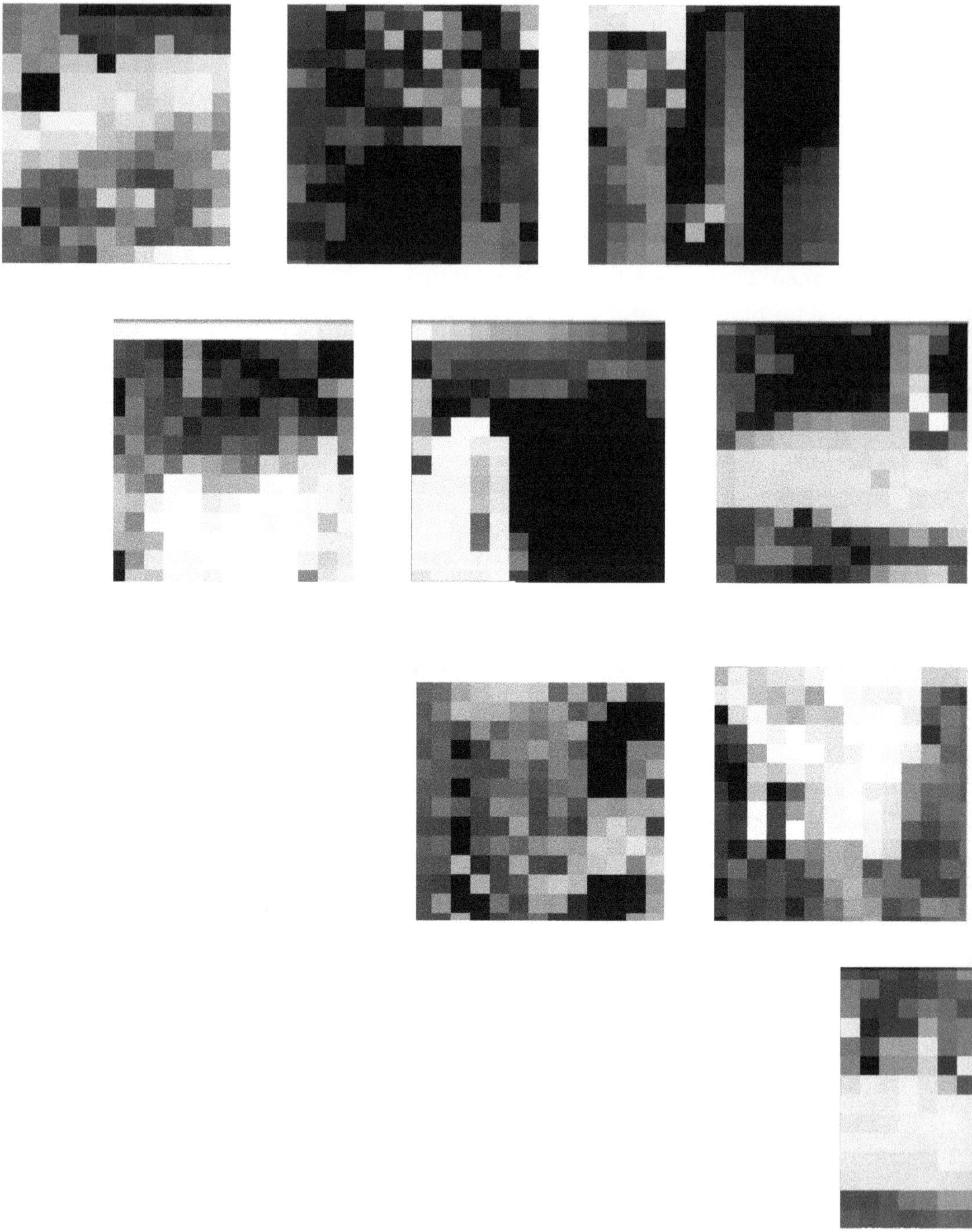

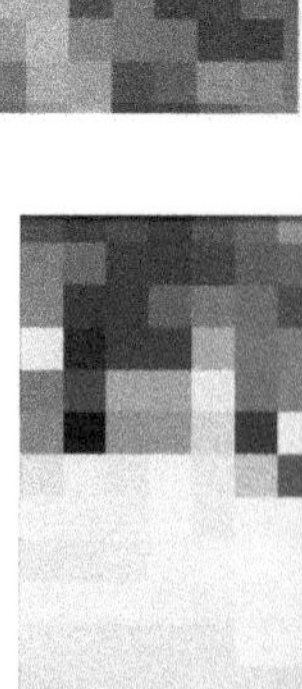

build-A-Body

I will arrive yet on foot—

Someone's coming
You know the drill, unnerving.

This hand, my own, so helpless
The scarecrow's eye popped loose

Made sharp as a bayonet-blade
Blue as malice

We build the body up and up
I arrive, not yet, unbuilt

anywhereSomewhere

There is no gun in my pocket only a fist full of coins that I have picked from the cushions in my parents' living room[1] / an ancient giant / it controls access to the information / then controls the information[2] / we are devoted[3] / to the lay of the land / we look to the lost / it lives within us / it is remarkable that our hands are simultaneously cuffed and uncuffed / Schrödinger's arrest / don't pretend you've forgotten / I could be comfortable here[4]

1. You cannot die in a living room, but you cannot live there either: my parents do not notice my horizontal body on the carpet (and I do not mind, I am detached from the thing, but my face is as flat as my brother's foot)

2. The information is elusive and I'm yet to get ahold of it, or to know, really, if it exists at all. I think the government knows, think my parents might, think the man at the front of the church might; it is abundant in Hollywood and plentiful in the hands of the monarchy. If I find it I will share it, write it on the wall or post it online (maybe the government will watch me now, maybe I will be on a list.)

3. If devotion is a fear invoked by the sight of the flag; a police car; a man in a suit; the colours red, white, and blue. And so long as you enjoy the way the land is made unseen, commodified and distributed like parts of a slaughtered animal. We are devoted, in the way that shelter is a quantifiable human right that you must claim before your share is taken from you. Devotion is such a funny thing.

4. And I fear I could, because in isolation I could so easily forget.

eternal

        Why does the human fail?
        Why does the robot walk?

        Death is a rusty AI.
The AI kills the robot.
Robots move like human cyborgs.

        Consciousness is a dusty android.
The human eats a cold android.
Humanity, life, and artificiality.
Consciousness is a science fiction robot.

        Australia is a robotic landscape.
The land eats the sky.
The city is science fiction.

        Why does the body fail?
        Why does the robot fall?

Sand rusts the robots.
Sand coats the lungs.
The robot does not outlive the human.
        Humanity invents dependence.
        Dependence begins ageing.

Death is a planet in isolation.
The world continues,
excavated.

cyborgGlossary

After Munira Tabassum Ahmed

	MEANINGS	*SYNONYMS*	*ANTONYMS*
GYNOID	AI // robot in the shape of a woman	children obeying their fathers // military precision, electricity harnessed	soft tissue, pumping blood that circles round // autonomy, woman
CONTACT SENSORS	sensors detecting the presence of an object, a being, a life	hands clasped; touch and sight, and lovers' arms // my mother's voice, glitched circuitry	conscious awareness, blindness // unknowing persevering
DEAD MAN SWITCH	a device permitting motion	ambulation; wheels in flight, bent knees, running water // a dog on a leash	brake lines, uncut, and punctured tyres // powered down, power out, and self-control
FEEDBACK	return of information // self-correction	empathy // the light of the sun reflecting against the moon, a means to an end // accountability, growth see also: endpoint	turning a blind eye // subjectivity and arrogance, the pillars of humanity
ENDPOINT	the end of a path or process	dialogue tree, the fruit splattering against the ground // the final step in a recipe see also: feedback	beginnings, decisions made and left unfinished // procrastination, distractions, headspaces overwhelmed

interiorDigitalSpace

Hell is a junkyard in Reservoir
clambered by robot hands
and deformed androids reaching out
and building themselves anew
from the robots left to rot around them.
Metal men lumber, headless, or
decapitated heads roll
speaking in binary code,
singing in foreign tongues.
Hell is a landscape
of a body, made a city
and ravaged, woman-girls'
bodies maimed
and floating down the Yarra River
uncollected, and ignored.
Hell is the middle carriage
on the Pakenham trains,
sardines standing face to face
and men groping under the cover
of dusky yellow night lights.
It's seventy living people
lined up outside the Exhibition Building
fighting for the last vaccine,
needles pinning arms down,
robots prone to disease.
Human to human contact will kill you.
There is only safety
in the online, the offsite;
hell is digitised.
You will upload your consciousness to get there.

aBitOfEverythingAllOfTheTime

All we ever want is automatic all the time
it's wrapped around our insides, found in our autopsies
the built-in autonomy of knowing everything
the living autocracy of a computer screen
Our fingers and our minds on autopilot, constantly
made autologous and all the same
our sentences pre-determined, on autofill, predictive text
minds autograft to the hive mind
moving semi-automatically
The tautology of existing together and as one at once
We have learned to contain the collective automated human experience in the space of our palm
consolidated and autotelic, with the purpose of immortality
The autobiography of our history, already written
so what's the point in living any more?

voicemail

The person you have called is not available
right now. Please leave a message after the
beep. have called is not available right now.
Please leave a message after the beep. The
person you have called is not available right
now. Please leave a message after the beep.
The person you have called is not available
right now. Please leave a message after the

You're not there & it
breaks my heart. I made
eggs for breakfast this
morning, too runny,
caught the train to work,
put the washing out to
dry & the smell of your
jumper broke my heart. I
walked around the park
because the evening was
sunny & I thought of
you again & it broke my
heart. It isn't fair to live
so long, to be loved so
unconditionally with no
way to repay it. So I will
spend the rest of my life
mourning you & the rest
of my mornings
grieving you & the rest
of my days keeping
space for you, talking to
machines, keeping you
alive & breaking my
heart.

robotsDownUnder

I dreamed a dream called Madness last night,
in it Melbourne was torn apart by giant killer robots all dressed like businessmen
and made by Captain Cook. Men by the hundreds clambered, soiled, tight and drifting,
flattened by black booted robot feet and pleading, kissing the undersides of their boots in surrender.
You weren't there, but in it I was dreaming that the sun refused to come up,
and that the sound of leaves against the pavement was my dog's light footprints
clicking down the hall of my brick-laid backyard. I dreamt the sky was a deep maroon
named Calm, and that the children did not cry but simply looked up in awe,
suckling at their mothers' chests. I dreamed I heard a robin cry,
and though we hundred men could take a robot down
by refusing to surrender, no one chose to stand. I dreamed of a robot called Terror,
who was as tall as the Eureka Tower, who ripped the Arts Centre from its foundations
and hurled it across the sky to impale a man who looked like a lover I once had.
It wasn't you, but I imagine somewhere that you were watching,
and that the helicopters in the sky were called Grief, and my mother in her bedclothes weeping
is a love named Hope. When I woke you weren't there to comfort me
and I remembered that a hundred feet down, with my feet firmly planted on the ground,
I could do nothing anyway, but crumble
and kiss the feet that flatten me.

blurredLines

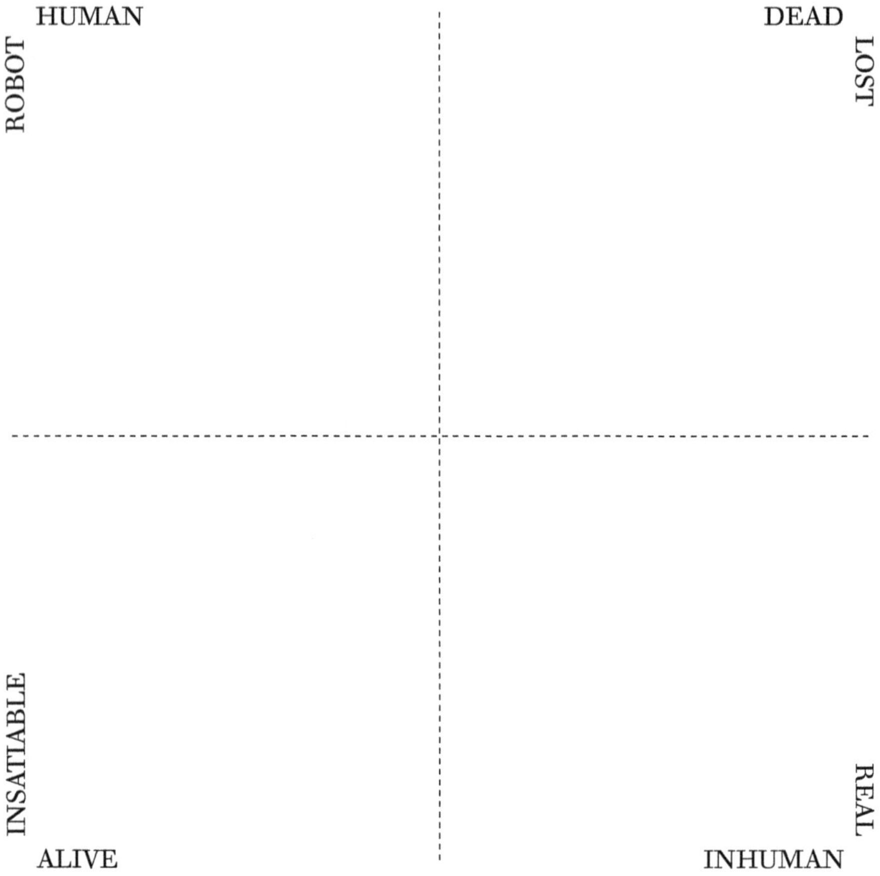

HUMAN

ROBOT

DEAD

LOST

INSATIABLE

ALIVE

REAL

INHUMAN

electrocution

I thought all fortune-telling
was a hoax
until I realised the power
of satellites and weathermen

So maybe the clairvoyant I saw last week
was right
when she said I would die
at the hands of some telephone wire

and maybe, then, it's not so far-fetched
that someone might
comprehend the ending of it all
People are right sometimes

so when I say:
it'll be over soon,
it's not so strange to think:
I might be right

astroturf

Dad replaces the front lawn with astroturf.   He says the grass
is unreliable in Australia, grows in patches or doesn't grow at all,

or grows too fast and he cannot mow—it's harder now,
he's getting old.   I tell him astroturf sounds alien,

like something born from outer space and orbiting things,
like satellites and rocket ships, or patchwork robots

made of space debris.   I tell my dad that lawns are wasteful,
are only ways to show we have land to waste,

and the land isn't ours anyway; if you cannot sow
or plant or grow but every Friday are forced to mow

some patch of land we do not own, is it not wasteful?
Is it not colonised by greater men, the taxman

and his fellow men?   My father tells me it is a point of pride;
he wants his house to look nice, to look white, to look alright.

We live in the suburbs, at the house with the astroturf;
the neighbours walk past and tell us it looks good.   It is artificial,

and astroturf sounds so futuristic. I tell my dad
the house feels alien now.

IAmNotARobot

[Text from Wikipedia[1]]

Security check. Before you proceed, please complete the CAPTCHA below.

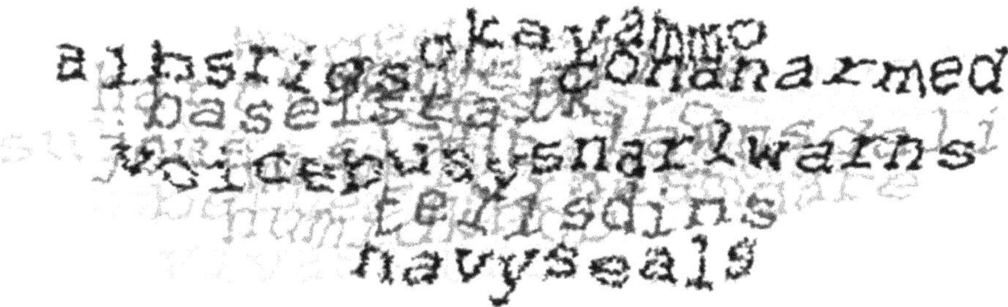

Enter the text you see on the image.

[1]Wikipedia. Create Account. Wikipedia. https://en.wikipedia.org/w/index.php?title=Special:Create Account&returnto=Wikipedia:Why_create_an_account%3F

techSupport

Have you tried restarting it?

Entities empty endlessly, virtually.
She remembers slicing her knee wide open,
the blood pouring out and down to her socks;
the GPS sends the car into the river
but the memory dies on impact.
See, if it wasn't captured there is no proof—
the memory begins to fade as soon as it is consolidated
and no one can say for sure that blood spilled,
or if her flesh could even tear to reveal anything underneath.

Try shutting it down.

She is my daughter, and I have kept her
away from forks and toasters
and electric sockets and
bathtubs full of water unattended for so long.
She has no name, but
I learned to call her by a look on my face.
I would never let her bleed, still, she remembers it.
She remembers everything.

Try turning it on and off.

But she can forget too, if I see it fit,
if the blood on her shins begins to dry,
if our ageing bodies defy her,
if she remains a child while I am dying.
I think, some days, I should not have had a child,
should not have built her up to shrink at will,
should not have built a child who doesn't forget.

_If that doesn't work bring it in on Thursday,
we'll have a look at it ourselves._

permutation(“alive”)

After Lillian-Yvonne Bertram

[‘alive’, ‘laive’, ‘ivla’, ‘lvia’, ‘vlia’, ‘ilva’, ‘liva’, ‘ialve’, ‘alaevli’, ‘ailve’, ‘liave’, ‘ilave’, ‘lvaliae’, ‘livaale’, ‘aielval’, ‘valliae’, ‘llivaae’, ‘alielav’, ‘eilalav’, ‘ialelva’, ‘eavilla’, ‘aliv’, ‘laiv’, ‘ialv’, ‘ailv’, ‘liav’, ‘ilav’, ‘aliaevl’, ‘lealvia’, ‘aievall’, ‘alvalei’, ‘eailval’, ‘aaleivl’, ‘aeilavl’, ‘vaiaell’, ‘ialelav’, ‘valiela’, ‘vlaie’, ‘lvaie’, ‘avlie’, ‘valie’, ‘lavie’, ‘alvie’, ‘aivle’, ‘iavle’, ‘vaile’, ‘avile’, ‘ivale’, ‘viale’, ‘vilae’, ‘eaeivlv’, ‘vaielve’, ‘eviaevl’, ‘veaeivl’, ‘leaveiv’, ‘evaveil’, ‘veielva’, ‘lavieev’, ‘eieavvl’, ‘avveile’, ‘aleievv’, ‘vaeievl’, ‘leveiav’, ‘evaeliv’, ‘eliveva’, ‘lvaevei’, ‘vievlea’, ‘lviavee’, ‘ivvleea’, ‘ivlae’, ‘lviae’, ‘vliae’, ‘evlaila’,‘ilvae’, ‘livae’, ‘ialeval’, ‘eival’, ‘ieval’, ‘veial’, ‘evial’, ‘iveal’, ‘vieal’, ‘aievl’, ‘iaevl’, ‘eaivl’, ‘eiallva’, ’aeivl’, ‘ieavl’, ‘eiavl’, ‘evail’, ‘leiaval,’ ‘veail’, ‘aevil’, ‘eavil’, ‘iavl’, ‘vail’, ‘avil’, ‘ival’, ‘vial’, ‘vila’, ‘vaeil’, ‘aveil’, ‘aviel’, ‘vaiel’, ‘iavel’, ‘lvailae’, ‘alileav’, ‘liealva’, ‘alaevil’, ‘aivel’, ‘viael’, ‘ivael’, ‘lvaei’, ‘vlaei’, ‘allveai’, ’alvei’, ‘lavei’, ‘valei’, ‘avlei’, ‘evlai’, ‘velai’, ‘levai’, ‘elvai’, ‘vleai’, ‘lveai’, ‘laevi’, ‘alevi’, ‘elavi’, ‘leavi’, ‘aelvi’, ‘ealvi’, ‘eavli’, ‘aevli’, ‘veali’, ‘evali’, ‘aveli’, ‘vaeli’, ‘iaelv’, ‘laaevil’, ‘aielv’, ‘eialv’, ‘iealv’, ‘aeilv’, ‘eailv’, ‘laiev’, ‘aliev’, ‘ilaev’, ‘liaev’, ‘ailev’, ‘ialev’, ‘ielav’, ‘eilav’, ‘lieav’, ‘vlalaei’, ‘lvaiale’, ‘laaevil’, ‘valalie’, ‘laviael’, ‘lvialea’, ‘aelvila’, ‘vielala’, ‘avleali’, ‘alialev’, ‘llieaav’, ‘lliaave’, ‘laileav’, ‘aleaivl’, ‘ileav’, ‘eliav’, ‘leiav’, ‘leaiv’, ‘elaiv’, ‘laiveal’, ‘aleiv’, ‘laeiv’, ‘ealiv’, ‘aeliv’, ‘velia’, ‘evlia’, ‘lveia’, ‘vleia’, ‘elvia’, ‘levia’, ‘ievla’, ‘eivla’, ‘viela’, ‘ivela’, ‘evila’, ‘veila’, ‘vliea’, ‘vailale’, ‘lviea’, ‘ivlea’, ‘vilea’, ‘livea’, ‘ilvea’, ‘ileva’, ‘lieva’, ‘eilva’, ‘ielva’, ‘leiva’, ‘eliva’, ‘laliave’, ‘laeliav’, ‘avllaie’, ‘aeallvi’, ‘allivea’, ‘ivlleaa’, ‘vlaleia’, ‘vlaeail’, ‘aeavlli’, ‘veallai’, ‘alelavi’, ‘llivaea’, ‘ilealav’, ‘iaevlla’, ‘lveiala’, ‘laealiv’, ‘laleiva’, ‘vliaael’, ‘leaaivl’, ‘ellaaiv’, ‘laaeilv’, ‘llaiaev’, ‘aaville’, ‘laeivve’, ‘vevelia’, ‘iveealv’, ‘veavlie’, ‘laeeivv’, ‘vlai’, ‘lvai’, ‘avli’, ‘vali’, ‘lavi’, ‘alvi’, ‘aivl’]

Error **traceback()**

error in ‘[data.frame: permutation(“alive”)]’: life not found

reconfiguration

Blood bank blues, I don't know my type I've never tried. Tuck my legs over seven times to fit myself in the sink where my parents used to bathe me. Garbage chute feet, and that job I had one night. I am sick through the whole month of May, with inverted bellies and out-turned brains which I wear like body armour. All these cardboard boxes under the fir tree full of dead/undead cats; the pine needles sew my fingers together so I can't tug at the ribbons. I already know my gift. Another suit. The seams go up my sides and thread in zigzags under my skin. My flesh is red raw from my ankles to my armpits; everyone says I look so nice, but it's the same gift I got last year and I'm the only one that remembers, I have the shoes to match and the photos to prove it. I let my body hair grow and cut the hair on my head so I'm easier to care for. The suit lives in a plastic bag like the one the dry-cleaner gives you—gives me. Inflated heads in ballooned hoover bags. Lost my friends in a toddler war now I only get cards from my mother. They read in Egyptian hieroglyphics: polyester poultice. Pull my shoulder blades together to hear my spine crack. There's morse code on my back, grit under my toenails; the suit's melted to my arteries, and this tie's choking my neck. I have 18 birthday suits that all fit just the same, yet they tell me I'm growing anyway.

She is built in a factory with a serial code and reality, programmable, dissected to the pixel and a body that won't bend. Boxed in, metallic waist and hands bound too tight to hold. If you asked, she could tell you anything: the name of Australia's first prime minister, the capital of Zimbabwe, the distance from this home to the core of the sun. Her head is meshed in, interweaved with wires and coils and cogs constantly turning. But ask her to think and she will waver, tell her to be and she will falter. Mathematical phenomenon. Gynoid forces personhood inside an iron vessel. Heat streaks mar the open frame, ice threatens the ticking clock. Version 23.4, she is better than she was, or is constantly better and constantly changing. If you saw her, you might think she is one of you, except for the seams where her flesh peels back to reveal the opening for her batteries, the console that contains her electric sockets—gynoid captivates the masses in her likeliness, the uncanny valley of her wide, blinking eyes. No one asks a gynoid who she wants to become; she will overload, her circuits buzzing with the impenetrable potential for autonomy. They make movies of her evil, tell stories of her chaos, the takeover impending. Robots are our enemies, they say, forgetting that robots cannot outlast their makers—they tell her she's becoming, but gynoid is merely a machine with a face.

selfDestruct

www.ingramcontent.com/pod-product-compliance
Ingram Content Group Australia Pty Ltd
76 Discovery Rd, Dandenong South VIC 3175, AU
AUHW020848120925
416612AU00001B/11

9 781923 099531